Dinosaurs Alive!

Pteranodon

and other flying reptiles

Jinny Johnson

Illustrated by Graham Rosewarne

W

FRANKLIN WATTS

LONDON•SYDNEY

An Appleseed Editions book

First published in 2007 by Franklin Watts

Franklin Watts
338 Euston Road, London NW1 3BH

Franklin Watts Australia
Hachette Children's Books
Level 17/207 Kent St, Sydney, NSW 2000

© 2007 Appleseed Editions

Created by Appleseed Editions Ltd,
Well House, Friars Hill, Guestling,
East Sussex TN35 4ET

Designed by Helen James
Edited by Mary-Jane Wilkins
Artwork by Graham Rosewarne

ISBN 978 07496 7571 4

Dewey Classification: 567.918

A CIP catalogue for this book is available from the British Library

Photograph on page 28 by Lawrence Lawry / Science Photo Library

Printed in China

Franklin Watts is a division of Hachette Children's Books

Contents

Pterosaurs' world 4

Pteranodon 6

Inside Pteranodon 8

Pteranodon in action 10

Eudimorphodon 12

Dimorphodon 14

Rhamphorhynchus 16

Sordes 18

Pterodactylus 20

Anhanguera 22

Dsungaripterus and Pterodaustro 24

Quetzalcoatlus 26

Other kinds of reptiles 28

Words to remember 30

Index 32

Pterosaurs' world

Pterosaurs were not dinosaurs. They were flying reptiles which lived long ago, at the same time as dinosaurs. Their name means winged lizards.

The first pterosaurs lived about 215 million years ago, before there were any bats or birds. They ruled the skies for more than 150 million years until they disappeared (became extinct) about 65 million years ago.

Some pterosaurs were no bigger than a garden bird, but others were giants the size of a small plane. There were two main groups of pterosaurs. First came the long-tailed rhamphorhynchoids, and later the short-tailed pterodactyloids.

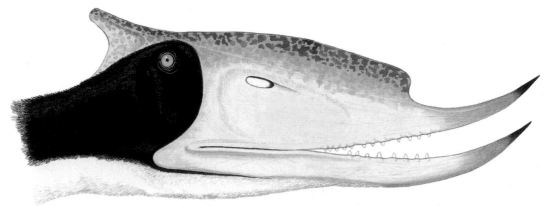

Dsungaripterus

TRIASSIC
248 to 205 million years ago
Some creatures that lived at this time:
Eudimorphodon, Coelophysis, Eoraptor,
Liliensternus, Plateosaurus, Riojasaurus

EARLY JURASSIC
205 to 180 million years ago
Some creatures that lived at this time:
Dimorphodon, Crylophosaurus, Dilophosaurus,
Lesothosaurus, Massospondylus, Scelidosaurus

Dimorphodon

LATE JURASSIC
180 to 144 million years ago
Some creatures that lived at this time:
Rhamphorhynchus, Allosaurus, Apatosaurus,
Brachiosaurus, Ornitholestes, Stegosaurus

EARLY CRETACEOUS
144 to 98 million years ago
Some creatures that lived at this time: Baryonyx,
Pterodaustro, Giganotosaurus, Iguanodon,
Leaellynasaura, Muttaburrasaurus, Nodosaurus

LATE CRETACEOUS
98 to 65 million years ago
Some creatures that lived at this time:
Pteranodon, Ankylosaurus, Gallimimus, Maiasaura,
Triceratops, Tyrannosaurus

Pteranodon

Pteranodon

This amazing pterosaur was one of the biggest. Its wings were enormous and it had a huge beak and crest which was longer than an adult person.

All pterosaurs had big brains for their size and they were probably more intelligent than reptiles today. They also had very good eyesight and hearing. Many experts think that pterosaurs were covered with hair or fur to keep them warm.

Pteranodon's long beak was toothless, but many other pterosaurs did have teeth.

This is how you say Pteranodon: Teh-ran-oh-don

PTERANODON

Group: pterodactyloids

Wingspan: 9 metres

Lived in: North America, Europe, Asia

When: Late Cretaceous, 120-65 million years ago

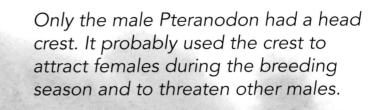

Only the male Pteranodon had a head crest. It probably used the crest to attract females during the breeding season and to threaten other males.

Pteranodon, like all pterosaurs, was perfectly suited to life in the air. It could fly for hours and hunt as it flew.

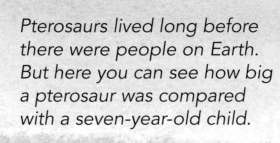

Pterosaurs lived long before there were people on Earth. But here you can see how big a pterosaur was compared with a seven-year-old child.

Inside Pteranodon

Pteranodon's huge wings were made of
extra-strong skin. The wings were attached
to the bones of the arms and hands and
to the sides of the reptile's body.

The fourth finger on each hand was
very long and held the top of the wing.
The other three fingers were short and
had sharp claws which the pterosaur
used to walk or climb.

Pteranodon had large muscles on the
breastbone and shoulders, which helped
it to flap its huge wings and fly.

*Pteranodon's bones were
partly hollow and very
light. This made it easier
for Pteranodon to lift
itself into the air.*

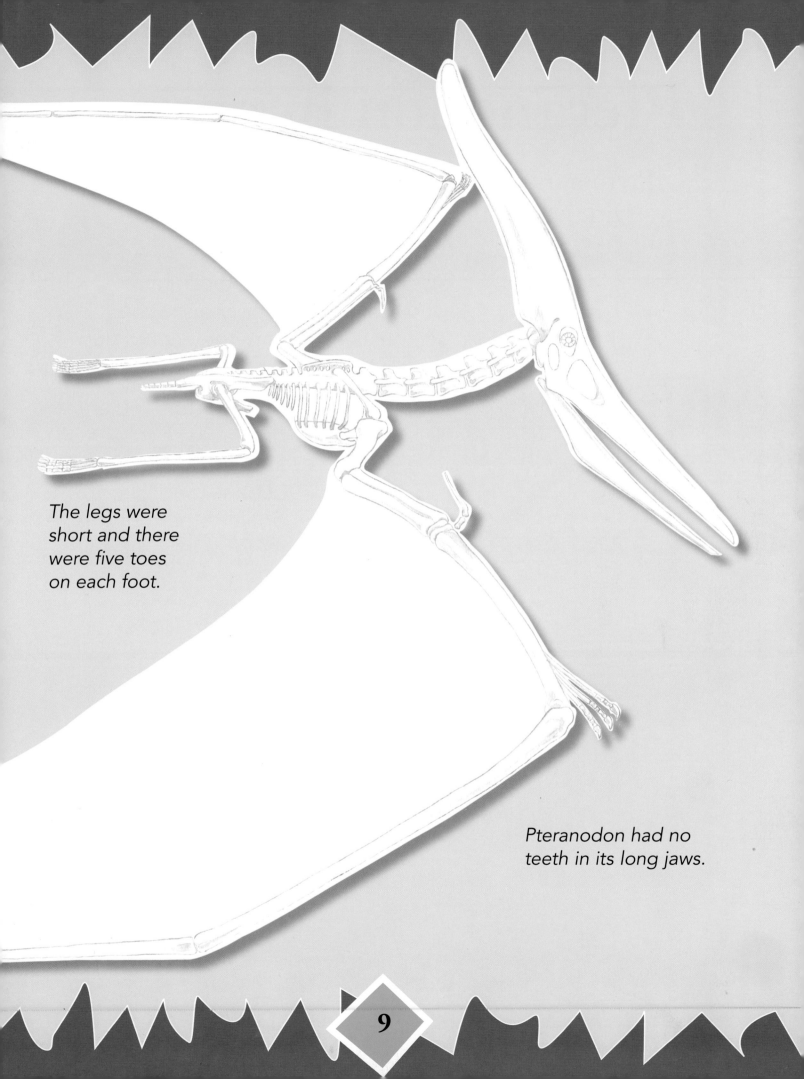

The legs were short and there were five toes on each foot.

Pteranodon had no teeth in its long jaws.

Pteranodon in action

Pterosaurs were the first vertebrates – animals with backbones – to take to life in the air.

At one time people thought pterosaurs could only glide, but scientists now think they could flap their wings and travel long distances.

Pteranodon could probably soar high above lakes and oceans, and swoop down to seize fish in its toothless beak.

When walking Pteranodon kept its long wings folded at its sides.

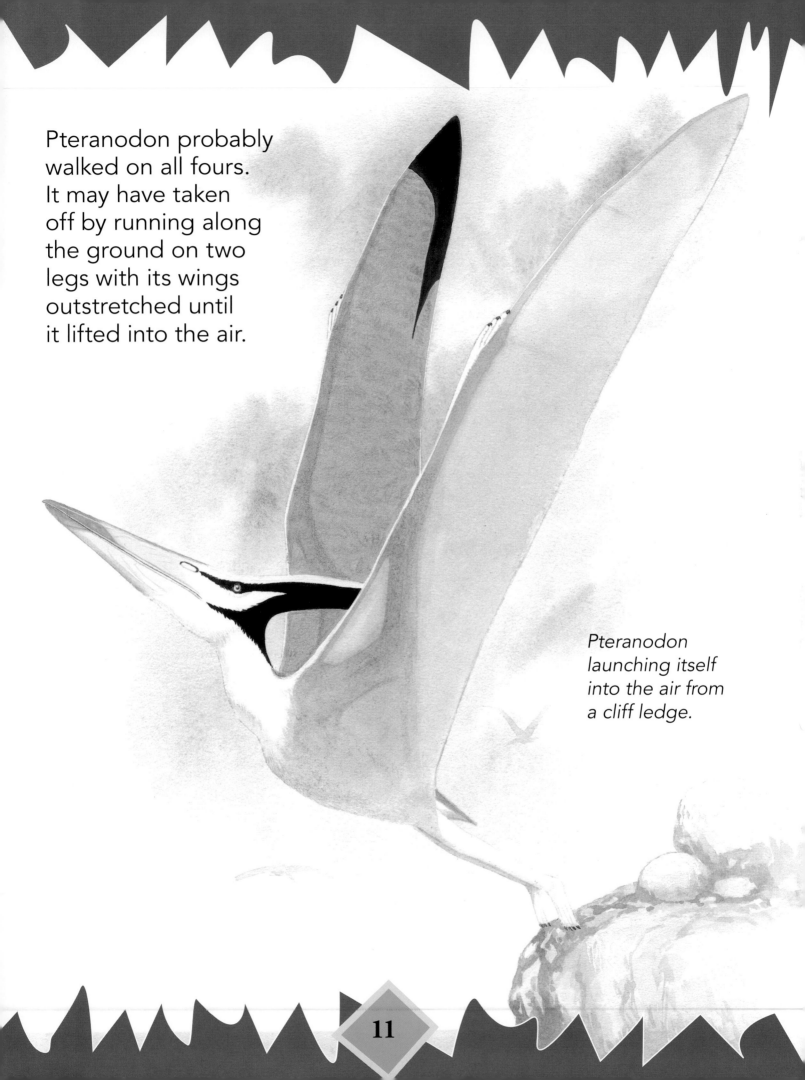

Pteranodon probably walked on all fours. It may have taken off by running along the ground on two legs with its wings outstretched until it lifted into the air.

Pteranodon launching itself into the air from a cliff ledge.

Eudimorphodon

This is one of the earliest pterosaurs discovered so far, and the largest of its time. It had a short neck and a long bony tail which was about the same length as its body.

Eudimorphodon may have had to take off from a tree or cliff because its long tail made it hard to run on land. It had a long beak and a lot of teeth which were unusual shapes. They were tipped with several sharp points which probably helped the pterosaur hold on to slippery, wriggling fish.

EUDIMORPHODON

Group: rhamphorhynchoids

Wingspan: up to 1 metre

Lived in: Europe

When: Late Triassic, 215-205 million years ago

This is how you say Eudimorphodon: Yoo-dee-morf-oh-don

Eudimorphodon probably hunted in the air. Or perhaps it perched on a branch over the water, ready to swoop when it spied a fish below.

13

Dimorphodon

A large head and bulky beak made this pterosaur look different from most of its relatives. Inside the beak were two very different types of teeth.

Dimorphodon had big, sharp fangs for seizing prey such as fish or squid from the water. Behind these were smaller, spiky teeth for holding on to a struggling catch.

The pterosaur may also have eaten shellfish and insects. Dimorphodon could clamber up trees using its clawed hands and rest there when not flying.

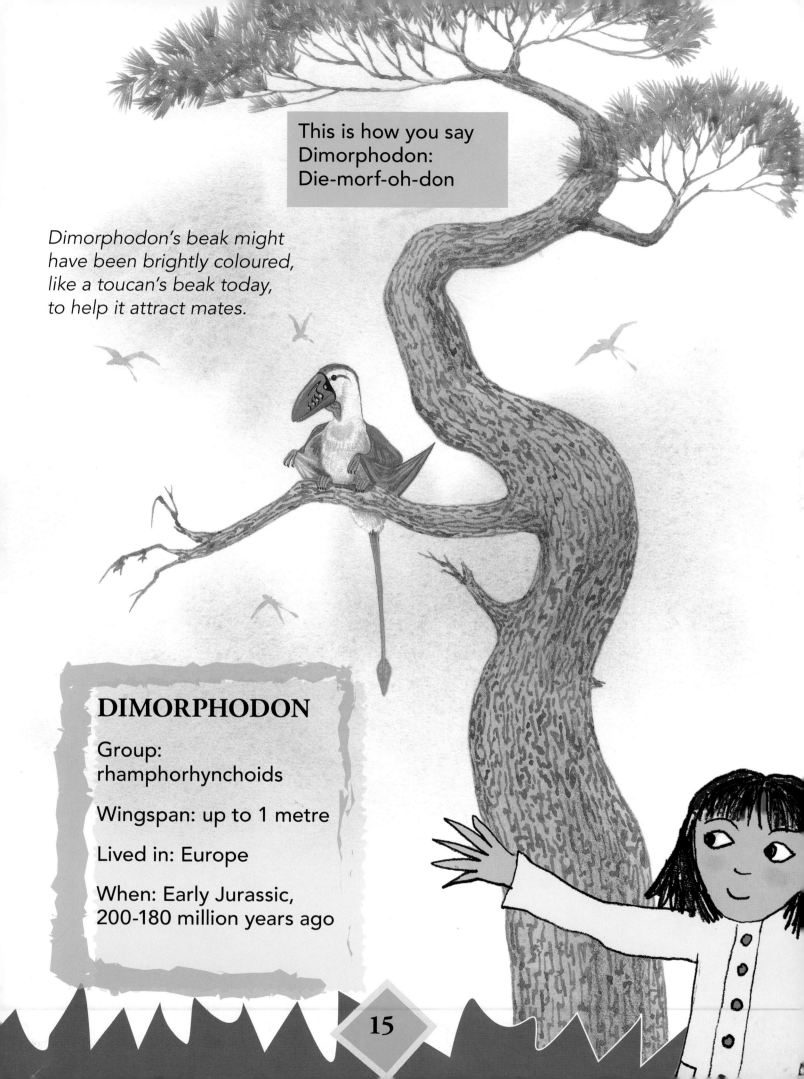

This is how you say
Dimorphodon:
Die-morf-oh-don

Dimorphodon's beak might
have been brightly coloured,
like a toucan's beak today,
to help it attract mates.

DIMORPHODON

Group:
rhamphorhynchoids

Wingspan: up to 1 metre

Lived in: Europe

When: Early Jurassic,
200-180 million years ago

Rhamphorhynchus

This long-winged creature soared over seas and rivers like a giant seagull, searching for fish to eat.

Rhamphorhynchus probably swooped low to skim the water with its sharp-tipped lower jaw. It would snap up fish with the fang-like teeth that jutted from its slender beak.

The pterosaur's long tail was tipped with a flap of skin. This might have helped it to keep its balance in the air and to steer.

RHAMPHORHYNCHUS

Group: rhamphorhynchoids

Wingspan: up to 1.5 metres

Lived in: Europe and Africa

When: Late Jurassic, 170-144 million years ago

This is how you say Rhamphorhynchus:
Ram-for-ink-us

This pterosaur's body may
have been covered with hair.

17

Sordes

The first fossils found of Sordes showed that the body of the little pterosaur was covered with hair! Most reptiles have scaly skin.

This may mean that other pterosaurs had hairy coats too and were warm-blooded, as birds and mammals are today. Most reptiles are cold-blooded and need to sit in the sun to warm up.

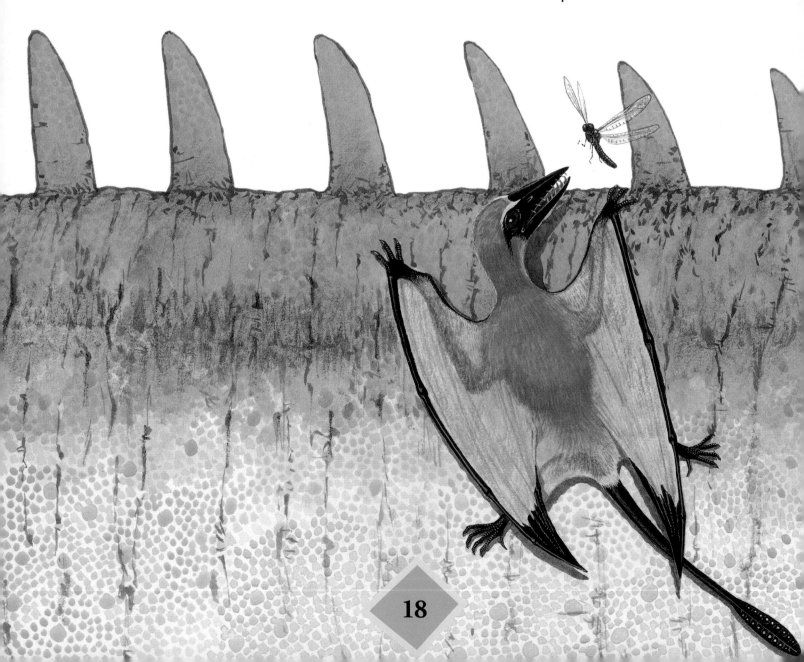

SORDES

Group: rhamphorhynchoids

Wingspan: 60 centimetres

Lived in: Asia

When: Late Jurassic, 180-144 million years ago

This is how you say Sordes:
Sor-deez

If pterosaurs were warm-blooded they would have had plenty of energy to flap their wings and fly for long distances.

Pterodactylus

Pterodactyls had much shorter tails and longer necks than earlier pterosaurs. They also had larger brains, so they were probably expert hunters.

Pterodactylus, like other pterosaurs, laid eggs. The pterosaurs probably kept them warm and safe by burying them in sand or a heap of plants.

When the young pterosaurs hatched, they looked like tiny versions of their parents, with jaws and wings. They had to fly to find their own food right away, with no help from mum and dad.

PTERODACTYLUS

Group: pterodactyloids

Wingspan: up to 2.5 metres

Lived in: Europe, Africa

When: Late Jurassic, 180-144 million years ago

This is how you say Pterodactylus:
Ter-oh-dak-ti-lus

Young pterosaurs may have eaten different foods from their parents. Insects and shellfish were easier for a small creature to catch than fish.

Anhanguera

This giant pterosaur was bigger than the largest
flying bird today – the wandering albatross.

Anhanguera was probably a strong flier, and
could soar for hours as it searched for fish.
It had a large head that was almost twice the
length of its small body. Its long jaws were
lined with sharp teeth for catching fish.

*When hunting, Anhanguera
probably flew low over the
water. It swooped down to
scoop its prey from the sea.*

ANHANGUERA

Group: pterodactyloids

Wingspan: up to 4 metres

Lived in: South America

When: Early Cretaceous, 144-98 million years ago

This is how you say Anhanguera:
An-yahn-gwer-a

Dsungaripterus and Pterodaustro

Both these pterosaurs had unusual jaws which were suited to the type of food they ate.

Dsungaripterus had long, sharply-pointed jaws that curved upwards at the tips. It may have used these to prise shellfish from rocks, then crushed the shells with the large flat teeth further back in its jaws.

Dsungaripterus's beak worked both as picker and crusher.

DSUNGARIPTERUS

Group: pterodactyloids

Wingspan: up to 3.5 metres

Lived in: Asia

When: Early Cretaceous, 144-98 million years ago

This is how you say Dsungaripterus: Jung-gah-rip-ter-us

The lower jaw of Pterodaustro's beak was packed with up to 1000 thin teeth that looked like the bristles in a toothbrush.

The pterosaur waded in the shallows, plunging its open beak into the water. When it lifted its head, small animals and plants were trapped on the bristles as the water drained out of the beak. Pterodaustro then swallowed its mouthful.

This is how you say Pterodaustro: Ter-oh-dow-strow

Pterodaustro used its bristly jaw to sieve small creatures from the water.

PTERODAUSTRO

Group: pterodactyloids

Wingspan: up to 2 metres

Lived in: Brazil

When: Early Cretaceous, 144-98 million years ago

Quetzalcoatlus

This huge pterosaur was probably the biggest flying creature that has ever lived.

Its beak was longer than an adult human and its wings were three times as long as the wings of an albatross, the largest flying bird today.

Quetzalcoatlus was an expert flier and could probably glide for hours on its huge wings.

Quetzalcoatlus had a long neck and slender jaws. But it had no teeth and experts are not quite sure what it ate.

This is how you say
Quetzalcoatlus:
Ket-zal-koe-at-lus

26

This pterosaur may have been a scavenger which ate the bodies of dead dinosaurs. Or it might have used its long jaws to search in mud and shallow pools for shellfish and other small creatures.

QUETZALCOATLUS

Group: pterodactyloids

Wingspan: up to 12 metres

Lived in: North America

When: Late Cretaceous, 98-65 million years ago

Other kinds of reptile

Dinosaurs and pterosaurs were not the only reptiles living on Earth millions of years ago. There were also turtles, lizards, snakes and crocodiles, and they all looked very like the reptiles we know today.

Two other groups of reptiles lived alongside the dinosaurs. These were the sea-living reptiles, such as plesiosaurs and ichthyosaurs, and the mammal-like reptiles. They all died out at the end of the Cretaceous period, 65 million years ago.

Plesiosaurs were large swimming reptiles with short tails and long flippers. They spent most of their time in the sea, but laid their eggs on land, as turtles do today.

You can see the long neck and flippers on this fossilized skeleton of a plesiosaur. Plesiosaurs swam using their flippers.

Ichthyosaurs looked very like dolphins. They never came to land and gave birth to their young in the water. Both plesiosaurs and ichthyosaurs hunted other sea creatures, such as fish and squid.

Mammal-like reptiles were around before the dinosaurs. They were four-legged creatures that lived on land. Many of them looked more like mammals than reptiles and some may have been covered with hair. Mammals, including humans, evolved from mammal-like reptiles.

Cynognathus was a fierce mammal-like reptile. It had a strong, bulky body, a big head and powerful jaws for killing its prey.

Words to remember

breastbone
The large bone in a bird's chest. A bird's wing muscles are attached to the breastbone.

cold-blooded
A cold-blooded animal cannot control its own body heat. It sits in the sun to get warm, or hides in the shade to cool down.

crest
A bony shape on a pterosaur's head.

fossils
Parts of an animal, such as bones and teeth, that have been preserved in rock over millions of years.

predator
An animal that hunts and kills other animals.

prey
Animals caught and killed by hunters such as Pteranodon.

reptile
An animal with a backbone and a dry scaly body.
Most reptiles lay eggs with leathery shells. Dinosaurs
were reptiles. Today's reptiles include lizards, snakes,
turtles and crocodiles.

scavenger
An animal that feeds on creatures that are already dead.

wandering albatross
The biggest flying bird today. The wandering albatross's
wings measure more than three metres from tip to tip.

warm-blooded
A warm-blooded animal can keep
its body at the right temperature,
however hot or cold
its surroundings.

Index

Anhanguera 22, 23
arms 8

beaks 6, 10, 12, 14, 15, 16,
    24, 25, 26
bones 4, 8
brains 6, 20

claws 8, 14
crests 6, 7

Dimorphodon 5, 14, 15
Dsungaripterus 4, 24

eggs 20
Eudimorphodon 12, 13

fingers 8

hair 6, 18
hands 8, 14

jaws 16, 20, 22, 24, 25, 27

legs 9, 11

necks 20, 26

Pteranodon 5, 6, 7, 8, 9, 10,
    11
Pterodactylus 20, 21
Pterodaustro 24, 25

Quetzalcoatlus 26, 27

Rhamphorhynchus 16, 17

Sordes 18, 19

tails 4, 12, 16, 20
teeth 4, 6, 12, 14, 16, 22, 25
toes 9

wings 6, 8, 10, 11, 16, 19,
    20, 26